Science and the Bible

Science and the Bible

30 Scientific Demonstrations
Illustrating Scriptural Truths

Donald B. DeYoung

Baker Books

A Division of Baker Book House Co
Grand Rapids, Michigan 49516

© 1994 by Donald B. DeYoung

Published by Baker Books
a division of Baker Book House Company
P.O. Box 6287, Grand Rapids, MI 49516-6287

Eighth printing, July 2000

Printed in the United States of America

Library of Congress Cataloging-in-Publication Data

DeYoung, Donald B.
    Science and the Bible : 30 scientific demonstrations illustrating scriptural truths / Donald B. DeYoung.
      p. cm.
    ISBN 0-8010-3023-4
    1. Bible and science—Miscellanea. 2. Activity programs in Christian education. I. Title.
BS652.D488 1994
220.8'5—dc20   93-21085

For information about academic books, resources for Christian leaders, and all new releases available from Baker Book House, visit our web site:
http://www.bakerbooks.com/

To **Jenny,**
who said,
"Don't give up, Dad."

Contents

List of Demonstrations

1. A large rainbow is made with an overhead projector.
   Gen. 9:13   Believing God's promises
2. An electric circuit is completed to light a bulb.
   Exod. 9:16   Using God's resources
3. A magnetic field is made "visible."
   2 Kings 6:17   Realizing God's power
4. Cans are crushed by the pressure of air.
   Job 28:25   Believing the Bible
5. Water glasses are made to ring.
   Job 35:10   Resting in the Lord
6. A volunteer is tied up with a cassette tape.
   Ps. 19:12–13   Forming good habits
7. One person wins a tug-of-war against several others.
   Ps. 46:1   Using God's resources
8. A person stands close to a heavy, swinging pendulum.
   Prov. 3:5   Trusting in God
9. Newspapers are torn in easy and difficult directions.
   Prov. 3:6   Choosing direction in life
10. Eggs are safely thrown at a target.
    Prov. 15:1   Controlling temper
11. Vinegar and baking soda blow corks from bottles.
    Prov. 19:19   Controlling temper
12. A bucket of water is safely swung in a circle.
    Prov. 29:25   Trusting in God
13. A balloon is suspended in the air with a hair dryer.
    Isa. 40:31   Using the Lord's strength
14. A tablecloth is quickly pulled from under a place setting.
    Matt. 24:40–41   Trusting in the Lord

15. Water is made to swirl from one bottle to another.
Mark 4:39   Turning to God

16. A boiled egg is pushed into an empty bottle.
Luke 11:24   Filling the heart with God

17. Two pendulums affect each other in a curious way.
John 13:35   Giving help and encouragement

18. A single sheet of paper is cut to make a large doorway.
John 20:19   Realizing God's presence

19. A paper card is cut into a seemingly impossible shape.
1 Cor. 13:12   Looking to the future

20. Rulers are dropped to measure short reaction times.
1 Cor. 15:51–52   Accepting the Lord

21. Nails are driven into a board held on a person's head.
Eph. 6:11   Protecting from evil

22. A ball is swung in a circle and then released.
Heb. 1:3   God controls the universe

23. One balloon is popped inside another one.
Heb. 4:12   Knowing ourselves

24. A comparison is made of hard water and soft water.
Heb. 4:13   Looking on the inside

25. A banana is sliced without being peeled.
Heb. 11:1   Understanding faith

26. A person swivels on a chair.
Heb. 12:1   Dropping things that hinder

27. A chain reaction is begun by igniting small dust particles.
James 3:5   Stopping gossip

28. A large object is moved with a very small one.
James 5:16   Prayer brings results

29. Objects are balanced in unusual ways.
2 Peter 3:17   Keeping steady in the Lord

30. A water balloon is heated without breaking.
Rev. 22:17   Accepting the gift of salvation

Introduction

This book contains thirty Bible and science activities. They have been used successfully with small and large groups of various ages. With help, children can also try most of the demonstrations at home in the kitchen. Most people have an interest in science, even if they are somewhat intimidated by it. The creation in all its wonder calls out to our hearts and minds for attention. In these activities science ideas are used to illustrate biblical truth. The Lord Jesus freely used everyday objects to communicate: rocks, water, sheep, and flowers.

One major danger with science demonstrations is that they may be remembered while the Scripture lesson is lost. The goal of the presenter should be to reverse this common problem. The demonstration should be like a compass that points back to the Scripture challenge. When a similar object is again seen by the listener, even weeks or years later, it can bring to mind the application of the related Bible lesson. For this reason, all the objects used in these demonstrations are familiar and readily available. Each lesson is divided into three parts: a Bible lesson, a demonstration, and a science explanation. The latter is provided for those who want further background information and should be integrated in the actual presentation. Deletions and additions are also encouraged. The lessons are purposely not written for word-by-word repetition. Any effective lesson must be adapted to the presenter's own style.

No effort is made in the lessons to cover every possible aspect of the Christian life. Instead, these particular lessons are chosen to be of practical help for all ages. Every lesson can be made evangelistic with a proper introduction and ending challenge.

The lessons are divided evenly between the Old and New Testaments. The New International Version of Scripture is quoted. If you have questions or comments about these activities, feel free to contact the author. It is my hope that this book will encourage the study and enjoyment of the Bible for all ages and that it will stimulate an awareness of the everyday details in God's creation that can illustrate biblical truth.

Ten Hints for Successful Science Demonstrations

1. Don't let demonstrations "steal the show." Start with a presentation of the Scripture. (Perfectly memorize it if possible.) Emphasize the main point of the lesson at the conclusion so the audience will clearly remember it.
2. Practice the demonstrations ahead of time. Repetition helps bring a smooth delivery, and practice avoids surprises when you are in front of the group. Prior practice prevents poor presentations!
3. Double check that all needed materials are present and arranged in convenient order. Small details add up to a confident and effective presentation.
4. Adapt demonstrations and Bible lessons to your own situation and talents. Improvise with available materials; insert new ideas of local or current interest. Creativity will hold the attention of your listeners.
5. When unexpected results occur in a demonstration, laugh and build them into your presentation. The audience will understand and be on your side.
6. Read the background of the Scripture passages. If you are comfortable and familiar with the Bible story, your confidence will be apparent.
7. Good demonstrations use everyday materials. When seen again months later, these items can trigger memory of the Bible lessons. Use of common items may also encourage the audience to try the demonstrations for themselves, extending the learning process.
8. Many of the best demonstrations involve a dramatic point: an unexpected result such as a popping balloon,

or something that brings "oohs" and "ahs." Science
demonstrations should be alive and exciting.

9. Have the audience participate as much as possible.
Instead of the lecture approach, help the listener be a
part of the Scripture lesson and demonstration.

10. Safety for you and the audience is the highest priority in
any science activity. Plan ahead for possible problems;
don't take chances. Know where a first aid kit is located.
If the demonstration involves a flame, have a fire extin-
guisher nearby.

1

Watch for the Rainbow

Theme: The rainbow is a reminder that God's promises do not fail.

Bible Verse: *I have set my rainbow in the clouds, and it will be the sign of the covenant between me and the earth* (Gen. 9:13).

Materials Needed:
  Overhead projector
  Clear plastic box
  Water
  Sheet of paper
  Tape

Bible Lesson

God placed a rainbow in the clouds at the end of the great flood in Noah's day. This was a visible sign of God's promise that there would never be another worldwide flood. A covenant is a firm agreement or promise between two parties. In this case, God reached out to the future generations of Noah and all living creatures and declared his love. Ever since the flood, local rainstorms have often been followed by beautiful rainbows. God remembers this rainbow promise after thousands of years, just as he faithfully keeps all the promises of his Word. Other favorite Scripture promises may be given or requested from the audience to enhance the lesson.

Science Demonstration

A rainbow appears when sunlight is dispersed into its many colors by water droplets in the sky. These rainbow colors always have the same order: red-orange-yellow-green-blue-indigo-violet. "Roy G. Biv" is a useful mnemonic for the order of colors. When all the colors are combined, the familiar white light appears.

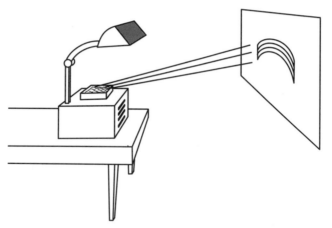

An overhead projector and a tray of water will project a large, colorful rainbow on a wall or screen. The shaded area on the upper portion shows where the lens should be covered.

An overhead projector can be used to produce a large rainbow. Instead of the usual glass prism, which produces a small unpredictable rainbow, a plastic box or tray works well. If possible, obtain a plastic shoe-storage box with a clear bottom. Otherwise, any clear glass container will also work. Pour three or four inches of water into the container and set it on the projector.

Be careful, since the water is on an electrical appliance. Next, cover up the front of the small upper projection lens with a sheet of paper and tape. When turned on, the machine's light will be bent and projected through the water. A large rainbow should appear on the wall or screen. The position of the rainbow can be adjusted by moving the container slightly or adding more water. The darker the room, the more easily the bow will be seen. An overhead projector bulb is actually designed to give a spectrum of colors similar to that of the sun. How closely does your indoor rainbow match God's glorious bow in the clouds?

Science Explanation

When white light passes between air and water, each color bends by a slightly different amount. This bending is called refraction and also occurs through glass prisms and other clear materials. The result is the dispersion of white light into its many component colors. In this demonstration the range of colors shown on the screen is determined by the nature of the projector bulb.

Refraction, or bending, occurs because the colors of light travel at different speeds through various clear materials. The color red travels slightly faster than violet light. In air or in a vacuum all the colors have the same speed.

Light is a complex subject, still not fully understood by scientists. The words *God is light* (1 John 1:5) remind us of our limited understanding of God.

2

Plug into God's Power

Theme: God's power is available to us if we are willing to reach out for it.

Bible Verse: *But I have raised you up for this very purpose, that I might show you my power and that my name might be proclaimed in all the earth* (Exod. 9:16).

Materials Needed:
Several batteries, C or D size
Flashlight bulbs, 3 volt
Six-inch lengths of wire, either insulated or bare

Bible Lesson

Moses was afraid to lead the Israelites out of Egypt. In Exodus 6:12 and 30, Moses told the Lord that he had faltering lips; he lacked power and confidence. However, the Lord promised to give Moses the words he needed to say. When Moses later stood before Pharaoh, the words of the Lord did indeed flow through him and Aaron. Moses thus became the leader of the entire nation of Israel. The above Bible verse actually refers to the raising up of Pharaoh, whom the Lord also used to reveal his great power (Exod. 9:16).

God's power is still available to us today if we are willing to live for him. We may not rule nations as did Moses or Pharaoh, but our daily walk can be an important testimony and encouragement to others. God's power can also help us live an upright life in an upside-down world. If we call on the name of the Lord Jesus to rule our lives, his power becomes ours. Let us follow Moses in obedience rather than follow Pharaoh in failure. A personal testimony of victory in Christ would be suitable at this point.

Science Demonstration

This activity is designed for individuals or small groups of two to four. Each person or group has a battery, bulb, and wire. The challenge is to make the bulb light up by connecting the three items correctly. The electrical energy is available within the battery; the trick is getting it to move through the bulb. Give no help as the teams try various combinations of circuits. In a few minutes, bulbs will begin to light up, and group members can then show each other how it is done. Of the many possible combinations, only a couple will result in light; most hookups are unsuccessful.

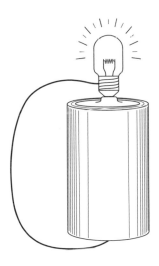

One possible arrangement that will light a flashlight bulb.

One caution: If the wire is connected directly across both ends of the battery and held there, the wire may become uncomfortably warm. This is called a short circuit. However, there is no shock hazard in the activity.

Science Explanation

To light the bulb, a series electrical circuit must be constructed. This requires a complete loop, including both ends of the battery and also both electrical contacts on the light bulb. The series circuit provides a complete conducting path for electrons to travel.

Electrons are the tiny electrical charges which produce power. When the bulb is lit, about ten million trillion (10^{19}) electrons pass through the filament each second. Electricity is part of the truly amazing world of microscopic particles.

3

God's Invisible Power

Theme: God surrounds and protects us with unseen power.

Bible Verse: *And Elisha prayed, "O LORD, open his eyes so he may see." Then the LORD opened the servant's eyes, and he looked and saw hills full of horses and chariots of fire all around Elisha* (2 Kings 6:17; see also 2 Kings 6:16 and Psalm 34:7)

Materials Needed:
   Magnet
   Iron filings, paper clips, or staples
   Dish with water
   A scrap of paper towel
   Needle or pin
   Overhead projector (optional)

Bible Lesson

The Arameans were warring against Israel. The enemy especially wanted to capture Elisha because he knew their military moves ahead of time. When Elisha's servant saw that the enemy had surrounded them, he panicked. Elisha declared that "those who are with us are more than those who are with them" (2 Kings 6:16). He then prayed that the ever-present power of the Lord would be revealed to this servant. Immediately the hills were seen to be filled with horses and chariots of fire. The enemy was ultimately turned aside by blindness (2 Kings 6:18–23).

Science Demonstration

There are many things in this world that are real even though we can't see them. Consider a small, permanent magnet. Completely surrounding this magnet is an invisible magnetic field. Put a sheet of paper over the magnet and sprinkle iron filings, staples, or paper clips on it, showing their alignment. (Do not let fine iron filings touch the magnet. They will be too hard to remove.) This also works well on an overhead projector screen, with the magnet placed under a transparency sheet. The invisible angelic powers that surround believers are just as real as the invisible magnetic field.

The earth also has magnetism that can be demonstrated. Float a needle in a dish of water by carefully laying the needle on a scrap of floating paper towel. Then sink the paper out from under the needle by pushing downward and soaking it. You may be able to float the needle directly by carefully lowering it into the water.

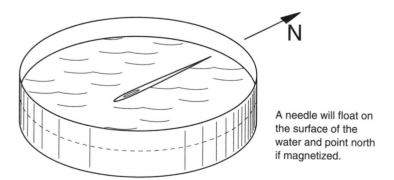

A needle will float on the surface of the water and point north if magnetized.

The needle will float because of the surface tension or "stickiness" of water; it should also orient itself to the north. Most needles and pins are naturally magnetized. (If not already magnetic, stroke the needle or pin a few times against a permanent magnet.) Rotate the needle slightly on the surface of the water and it will again return to the north direction. This works well for larger groups by using an overhead projector and a water dish with a clear bottom. A real compass can also be used to show the earth's magnetism, but this homemade floating compass is more interesting.

Just as the invisible angels protected Elisha and his servant, the earth's magnetic field also keeps us from harm. Radiation constantly flows toward the earth from the sun in what is called the solar wind. This wind of high-speed particles would harm us if the earth's magnetism didn't deflect the particles and prevent them from hitting us. Instead, their path is bent to the far north and south where they harmlessly enter the polar regions of the earth. There they sometimes give a glow to the atmosphere, which causes the aurora, or northern and southern lights. We are surrounded by a number of invisible shields, including magnetism and the ozone layer. Even greater is the divine protection that the Lord revealed to Elisha and his servant long ago.

Science Explanation

The surface tension of water allows a needle, a razor blade, or a water bug to float directly on the liquid surface. Surface tension is unusually high for water, compared with most other liquids. Within a water molecule (H_2O), a hydrogen atom (H) that is covalently bonded to an oxygen atom (O) is also attracted to surrounding oxygen atoms. The separate water molecules in a sense "hold hands" as they attract each other. This results in the high surface tension of water.

Surface tension reveals itself in many ways. It causes the spherical shape of rain, fog, and cloud droplets. It also causes fluid to cling to our joints for internal lubrication. In addition, surface tension explains how sap is able to climb upward in trees, as water molecules pull upward on one another. Without water's outstanding cohesiveness, trees could not possibly grow tall. Flowers and plant leaves would also be in trouble. It is the changing water pressure within tiny capillaries that causes leaves to fold by night and opens blossoms by day. In many ways water is a very special and essential resource.

4

The Weight of Air

Theme: The Bible is accurate in every single detail, including scientific ideas.

Bible Verse: *When [God] established the force of the wind and measured out the waters . . .* (Job 28:25).

Materials Needed:
Glass of water
Paper plate or index card
Hot plate
Empty pop cans
Pot holder or tongs
Tray of cool water

Bible Lesson

In this technical age it is often assumed that the Bible is out-dated and prescientific in its content. After all, Scripture was written more than two thousand years ago, long before modern scientific discoveries. In truth, however, God's Word is found to be entirely accurate, even in the smallest details.

Job 28:25 declares that God established the earth's wind and water. The entire chapter describes the source of real wisdom: knowing the Creator who made all things. The "force of the wind" ("weight for the winds" in the King James Version) is a phrase that accurately describes the heaviness of air. If air had no weight, then the wind could have no force. If this were the case, barometers would read zero pressure. Instead, the air above us exerts an average pressure of 2,100 pounds upon each square foot of surface, or about fifteen pounds per square inch. Job 28, written long before the modern concept of pressure, is entirely correct in referring to the force or weight of the wind. The Bible is indeed trustworthy in every detail.

Science Demonstration

There are several ways to demonstrate air pressure or the weight of air. Two interesting methods will be described here. First, fill a glass with water, perhaps from a pitcher. Place a paper plate or index card over the top, and while holding it in place, tip the glass upside down. Now take your hand off the card, and it should stay in place. The pressure of the air, actually pushing upward from underneath, is greater than the downward weight of the water in the glass. This demonstration works whether the glass is full or only partially full of water. You must take care that the paper maintains a good seal, and do not tilt the glass. Practice this over the sink.

The second method requires some preparation ahead of time. Pour one to two inches of water into several empty aluminum pop cans and set them on a hot plate. The water needs to be heated to the point of gently boiling, with steam rising from the openings. When ready, pick up a can with a pot holder or small tongs and tip it upside down into the tray of water. This will seal the open end of the can below the water level and will also quickly cool the steam inside the can. As the steam condenses, a vacuum develops within the can. The weight of the outside air will then rapidly crush the can with a loud snapping sound. Repeat the demonstration with the other cans, or let volunteers

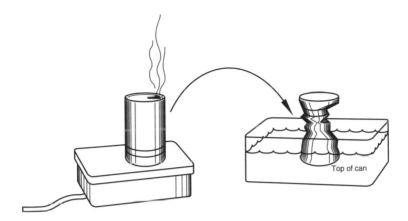

Water is brought to a boil in a pop can. When the can is
inverted in a tray of water, it is crushed by air pressure.

try the technique. The weight of the air, referred to in the Book
of Job, acts as a can crusher.

Science Explanation

It may seem that the air is entirely weightless. However, each
cubic foot of air actually weighs about one-tenth of a pound.
The air in a typical room thus adds up to several hundred
pounds.

Air exists for several miles above the earth, gradually thin-
ning with altitude. Gravity attraction keeps this air "attached" to
earth. It is the weight of this air layer that results in atmospheric
pressure on the earth. The pressure exists in all directions; hence,
it pushes upward on the card under the glass as well as against
the sides of the pop cans in the demonstration.

Why are our bodies not crushed by the ever-present air pressure? We are not affected because we are an "open system." By
breathing air, we maintain largely the same pressure inside as
outside our bodies. If we dive deeply into water, we quickly
feel additional pressure from the weight of the water above us.

5

Singing Glasses

Theme: God gives his children precious comfort in times of trouble.

Bible Verse: *But no one says, "Where is God my Maker, who gives songs in the night?"* (Job 35:10).

Materials Needed:
Several goblets
Water

Bible Lesson

The passage in Job 35 describes those who do not call upon God for help. They may cry out and plead for aid (v. 9), but they ignore the one source of help available to them. Let us be sure that we do not fail in this way. Instead, we have the privilege of calling upon the name of the Lord in times of trouble.

Nights especially can be times of fear and loneliness. This is when the presence of the Lord is most precious, as he "gives songs in the night." Such a song may be a Bible verse or an actual chorus or hymn. Perhaps we take Christian music too much for granted. It is a great blessing; our lives would be diminished without it. Remember Paul and Silas, who were comforted with songs at midnight while they were locked in prison (Acts 16:25). The Lord and his disciples also sang a hymn before they went to the Mount of Olives, where Jesus was arrested (Matt. 26:30).

A moist finger rubbed around the rim can cause a goblet to ring.

Science Demonstration

Set out several goblets (drinking glasses with stems) with water in them. Ordinary drinking glasses may also work, but not as well. The secret is to have glassware with thin walls.

By themselves the glasses are silent; they have no ability to make music. However, the touch of a finger can make them sing. Wet your index finger and gently stroke the goblet completely and continuously around the rim while you hold the glass steady by the base of the stem. Very little finger pressure is needed, and the finger must be kept moist while it is moving around the rim. In a few seconds the glass should start to resonate or vibrate, causing a clear, loud sound. The ringing sound is quite pleasant. The pitch, or frequency, depends on the glass size and also on the amount of water it contains. Volunteers may want to help you get several goblets vibrating at the same time. By adjusting the water levels, interesting chords can be produced. It takes a gentle hand to coax the sounds from the glasses. Likewise, it takes the Lord to give comforting "songs in the night."

Science Explanation

The ringing of a glass is called a resonance vibration. Sound is always produced by vibrating objects, whether violin strings, vocal chords, or air currents within a flute. For a goblet, the moving finger causes the sides of the glass to vibrate slightly inward and outward. The moistened finger provides a smooth contact, necessary for the continuous sound. It is somewhat like a violin bow moving across a string and causing the string to vibrate.

The sound produced by a goblet has a frequency of several hundred cycles per second. If you watch the water surface closely, you will see tiny standing waves produced by the moving glass walls.

Goblets can sometimes be shattered by high-frequency sounds that originate outside themselves. This is also called resonance, but it is an entirely different type of vibration. The shattering frequency is well above 20,000 cycles per second and very loud. The atoms within the glass begin to vibrate violently and eventually tear apart, resulting in breakage.

6

Bad Habits

Theme: Make sure your habits are positive so they will be a strength rather than a weakness, and rely on God's strength to break bad habits.

Bible Verses: *Forgive my hidden faults. Keep your servant also from willful sins; may they not rule over me* (Ps. 19:12–13).

Materials Needed:
An old audiocassette tape
A volunteer

Bible Lesson

David prayed that God would forgive and protect him from two kinds of sin: "hidden faults" and "willful sins." Hidden faults are problems that we may not be aware of. These weaknesses, or bad habits, can become such a part of our lives that we don't notice their effects. Willful sin is disobedience that we are aware of and make a conscious decision about. Either kind of sin is a failing before God that needs our confession and his forgiveness, just as David prayed.

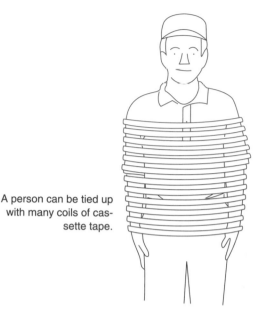

A person can be tied up
with many coils of cas-
sette tape.

Science Demonstration

This lesson calls for a volunteer to stand before the group. The tape in an old cassette represents a fault or problem. Wrap the tape around the person a couple of times, with his or her arms down. Ask the person to break loose from the "fault," which is easily done by spreading the arms and breaking the ribbon of tape.

When a sin is repeated often, it becomes a habit that is hard to break. Repeatedly wrap the cassette tape around the person's arms while you talk, until the tape is all used: ten, twenty, or thirty times around. Now ask the person to again break free, a more difficult task than before. The small strength of each individual section of tape now combines with the others to add up to a confining barrier. Likewise, bad habits can completely take over a person's life. Finally, carefully cut through the strands with scissors to represent God's power through prayer. There is freedom from bad habits, with the Lord's help.

Science Explanation

A ninety-minute cassette tape holds about 450 feet of plastic ribbon. A single strand can be broken easily like a thread, especially by snapping it. Suppose, however, that a person is wrapped twenty times around by the ribbon. It will take twenty times as much force to break loose, and the snapping motion is no longer possible. Usually the many sections will stretch slightly without breaking at all.

Many small sections add up to a strong barrier. Further investigation of strong cords or ropes will show that they are made up of weak individual threads.

7

The Lord's Strength

Theme: When we are on the Lord's side, his strength is available to us.

Bible Verse: *God is our refuge and strength, an ever-present help in trouble* (Ps. 46:1).

Materials Needed:
A length of clothesline, about 25 feet long
Two sturdy broomsticks or poles
Two or more volunteers

Bible Lesson

People are very interested in improving their health and strength. Physical fitness centers prosper everywhere. These efforts are commendable, but physical strength is only temporary. How quickly it fades with age. In contrast, the Lord's strength is permanent and readily available to us. This does not necessarily mean he gives us the ability to win races or lift weights. God's refuge and strength help us to have victory over the pressures of life. Especially when troubles arise, the Christian has spiritual resources: prayer, the Bible, and Christian friends. By trusting in Christ, we exchange our own limited strength for that of the Creator of the entire universe.

Science Demonstration

This demonstration shows how one person's strength can be greatly increased. It reminds us of extra strength that is available from the Lord. The activity requires at least two volunteers. You will show that you are stronger than both of them combined.

Have the two volunteers stand facing one another, each holding a sturdy broom. After tying one end of a smooth rope (one that slides easily) to one of the broomsticks, loop it around both

Two broomsticks are loosely wrapped with rope. One person can outpull several others by pulling on the end of the rope to draw the sticks together.

sticks, keeping them about two feet apart. Now have the volunteers pull outward on the broomsticks. When you pull steadily on the free end of the rope the sticks should be drawn together, regardless of how hard your volunteers resist. The feat should also work well with four volunteers pulling against you.

You have actually made a block-and-tackle system, long used to gain what is called a mechanical advantage. Your pulling force is multiplied by the number of loops around the broomsticks; your volunteers don't have a chance. With a strong rope and the right arrangement of pulleys, it is possible to pull a car up a hill or even pull down a tree. Just as you gain an advantage with the rope, the Lord's strength gives an advantage during difficult times.

Science Explanation

Suppose you and the four volunteers can each pull with a force of fifty pounds. Each broomstick will then be pulled outward with one hundred pounds. If there are five turns of rope around the sticks, your force will be multiplied to 250 pounds (5 x 50). Thus you have a 150-pound advantage. Some of this advantage will be lost because of friction of the rope. If this loss is small, you can still easily outpull the volunteers.

Notice that two of the four volunteers are not really necessary. The experiment would be the same if one broomstick were permanently attached to a wall. By Newton's third law of motion, the wall will pull back (reaction) with a force equal to that of the volunteers (action force). However, the four struggling volunteers give a more impressive demonstration.

This demonstration does not defy the conservation or constancy of energy. Instead, the advantage of a greater force is gained at the expense of a longer length of pull. As you draw the two broomsticks together, you will accumulate a coil of rope at your feet.

8

A Swinging Hammer

Theme: Believers should experience a growing trust in the Lord in all circumstances of life.

Bible Verse: *Trust in the LORD with all your heart and lean not on your own understanding* (Prov. 3:5).

Materials Needed:

A hammer or other heavy object

A strong cord and some way to attach it to the ceiling

Bible Lesson

Trusting in the Lord is easy until the time of testing comes. When difficulties arise, then the real test occurs: Will doubt and fear take over, or will prayer and trust shine through? All Christians fail this test now and then. Their natural reaction to stress is to try to solve their problems in their own limited strength.

Our understanding of problems is limited. We often think that the worst will happen, and then panic sets in. In such cases we ignore the greatest resource we have available, the power of God. We should remember that he remains in control of every situation. Fear and worry can be safely turned over to God.

Problems can then be seen as valuable lessons for Christian growth. It takes lifelong effort to allow the Lord fully into our everyday trials. The more we trust God in all things, the greater will be our enjoyment of life.

Science Demonstration

Hang a heavy object from the ceiling by a cord at about chest level. The higher the ceiling, the better will be the result. If the room has a suspension ceiling, tie the cord to a plant hanger, a removable hook attached to the metal ceiling frame. The object should swing in a smooth arc like a pendulum. Do not allow it to spin wildly.

According to the laws of motion and energy, a pendulum can never swing higher than its initial height at the time of release. In fact, it will lose a little bit of height on each swing because of air resistance. You or a volunteer can demonstrate trust in natural

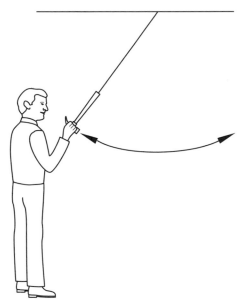

One person stands just beyond the swing of a heavy pendulum. The weight cannot move higher than its beginning height.

laws. Hold the weight off to the side, close to your nose. Then release the weight and let it swing through a broad arc. It should return very close to your nose but not quite touch you. Important: You must initially release the weight from rest without pushing on it. When the weight returns on its backswing, you will have a strong tendency to duck out of the way. This fear results from your limited understanding of the apparent danger. However, the swing of a correctly released pendulum has never been seen to break either the laws of nature or a nose.

Every day we trust our lives to natural laws. We travel at high speed in cars or planes. We handle electric switches without fear of shock. We walk across floors, believing they are strong enough to support us. How much greater should be our trust in the Lord, who established the very natural laws we live by.

Science Explanation

A pendulum alternates its energy between potential energy (position) and kinetic energy (motion). At each end point of its swing, a pendulum's motion momentarily ceases and all the energy is potential.

Energy is always conserved or constant in nature. It can be neither created nor destroyed. This is the most fundamental natural law, sometimes called the first law of thermodynamics. For this reason, a pendulum cannot swing higher than it is initially raised.

Conservation of energy makes the world a dependable place in which to live. Without it pendulums would swing erratically, sunshine would be unpredictable, and airplanes would fall from the sky. Colossians 1:17 declares that God continually upholds the laws of his creation. Thus they are entirely dependable.

9

A Straight Path

Theme: With the Lord's help we can have purpose and direction in life.

Bible Verse: *In all your ways acknowledge him, and he will make your paths straight* (Prov. 3:6).

Materials Needed:
Sheets of newspaper
Several volunteers

Bible Lesson

People on the Lord's side have straight paths. Not that this present life is perfect, but the Lord helps us continually to make choices and handle life's problems. In God's strength we can go forward with confidence that he leads us along. We talk to him in prayer and obey his Word, the Bible. In this way we will learn which paths to travel and which choices to make. In times of special need we can call upon his name for help. How sad to neglect the greatest resource available on earth.

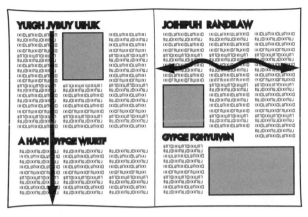

A newspaper will tear straight in a downward direction (left) but unevenly across the page (right).

Science Demonstration

How about a paper-tearing contest? Give several people full sheets of newspaper. Tell one group to tear off narrow strips from top to bottom, perpendicular to the writing. The second group must tear the newspapers across the page, parallel to the printed lines. The contest is to see which group produces the neatest straight strips. It will soon be apparent that the second group has great difficulty. Have fun coaching this group, encouraging them to do better.

Newspapers generally tear much more easily down the page than across. A newspaper has internal wood fibers that are lined up in the direction in which the paper was rolled during manufacturing. These cellulose fibers are somewhat like invisible threads within the paper. The paper tears easily and relatively straight along this aligned direction. Against this grain, however, it is almost impossible to tear a straight line for any length. Those on the Lord's side have direction and purpose, like the straight strips of paper. Those who ignore the Lord, however, are headed for trouble and frustration, like trying to evenly tear paper the hard way—against its internal grain.

Science Explanation

Papermaking techniques go back nearly two thousand years. Wood material is typically ground up and reduced to a slurry of loose fibers. This pulp then receives additives such as glue, clay, and color pigments. These additives determine the type and quality of paper.

The liquid pulp is spread onto a conveyer belt. It is then pressed flat, dried, and smoothed. In this process the internal fibers tend to align themselves in the direction of movement of the paper. For this reason a newspaper usually has a preferred direction of tearing. Individual wood fibers can often be seen within the newspaper sheet, especially if it is held up to light.

The manufacture of notebook paper or stationery involves a finer grinding of wood fibers and additional filler materials. These types of paper will tear equally well in any direction.

10

Turning Away Anger

Theme: We can control the outcome of arguments if we have self-control.

Bible Verse: *A gentle answer turns away wrath, but a harsh word stirs up anger* (Prov. 15:1).

Materials Needed:
A large piece of cloth (sheet, towel, tablecloth)
An egg
Three volunteers

Bible Lesson

People have a natural desire to answer harsh words with more of the same: "He can't get away with saying that, especially when I am right and he is wrong!" However, such heated arguments will only increase the problem instead of solve it. The proverb in this lesson gives a better approach: Disarm your opponent by controlling your own emotions. There is no more effective strategy than listening to the other side of the issue and honestly trying to understand it. A gentle answer might include an apology or just a willingness to listen. This approach certainly reflects a Christ-like spirit and is a testimony to others.

Science Demonstration

In this demonstration someone forcefully throws a fresh egg at close range at a vertically suspended cloth held up by two brave volunteers. The bottom of the cloth is folded up to form a pocket, held in place by the volunteers. When the egg hits the loosely held cloth, there is enough "give" to safely slow down the egg without breaking it. The egg then slides harmlessly down the cloth and into the pocket below.

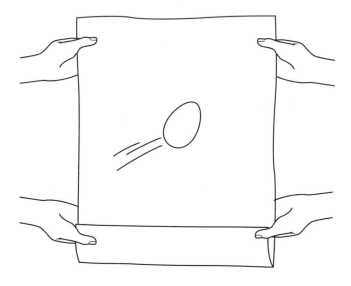

A suspended cloth sheet with a pocket formed at the bottom will safely catch a thrown egg.

The egg could now be dropped onto a hard surface and broken to show that it is delicate and raw. The extended lesson is that a mishandled egg, like uncontrolled anger, has damaging results.

Science Explanation

The technique with the cloth is similar to playing catch with bare hands. As you catch the ball, you can move your hands with the ball as you receive it to spread out the impact time and lessen the sting of the catch. The longer the stopping time, the smaller the resulting force. Likewise, the sheet slows down the moving egg in a way that protects it from breaking.

This slowing technique is the opposite of batting a ball. When a bat connects with a ball, the ball experiences a large force. As home-run hitters know, one secret of success is a fast swing.

By Newton's second law of motion the force needed to stop a moving object depends directly on how quickly the object is stopped. If an object strikes a hard surface, it may stop instantly and experience an enormous force. If the object can be decelerated more slowly, however, the force needed to stop it is greatly reduced.

Automobiles are designed with Newton's second law of motion in view. The bumpers are designed to "give" in a collision, lengthening the impact time and also absorbing the blow. A car's steering wheel and dashboard are also padded to lengthen impact time and thus soften bumps to the head. In an emergency an airbag likewise protects a person during sudden deceleration.

Isaac Newton studied motion three centuries ago. He would probably have preferred that his conclusions be called God's laws rather than Newton's laws. He strongly believed that the Creator had established the rules of the physical world.

11

Popping the Cork

Theme: An uncontrolled temper is foolish and also dishonors the Lord.

Bible Verse: *A hot-tempered man must pay the penalty; if you rescue him, you will have to do it again* (Prov. 19:19).

Materials Needed:
Pop bottles with corks
Vinegar
Baking soda
Short length of ribbon (optional)

Bible Lesson

An uncontrolled temper often leads to improper words and actions. The results may include unwise decisions and broken friendships. Whatever the eventual penalty, it is usually worse than the initial problem that caused the temper tantrum in the first place. Sadly, as the Bible verse explains, a hot-tempered person does not easily learn patience. Instead, he repeats the same error again and again.

46

We all have seen examples of a hot-headed person, many of them humorous. He kicks his lawnmower when it won't start, hurting his foot; he breaks his golf club over his knee after a bad putt; he slams the door, and a picture on the wall shatters. Actually, there is a more serious side to losing one's temper, especially for the Christian. The habit reveals a loss of self-control and discipline. Instead of letting the Spirit of Christ lead, the person allows the sinful nature to take over. Losing one's temper is definitely not a good testimony.

The cure to the temper problem is found in Proverbs 15:1: "A gentle answer turns away wrath, but a harsh word stirs up anger." A gentle answer is the exact opposite of a temper outburst. It leaves no room for uncontrolled anger if it is sincere. For further discussion of temper, see the lesson based on Proverbs 15:1.

Science Demonstration

Uncontrolled temper will be illustrated by pressure built up inside a bottle. Line up several pop bottles, perhaps tilted toward the audience but not pointed directly at them. Into each bottle pour a cup of vinegar. At demonstration time put two tablespoons of baking soda into each bottle and plug the ends with corks. To delay the reaction, the baking soda can be wrapped up in small pieces of bathroom tissue. As the paper moistens, bubbling will start. The chemical reaction between

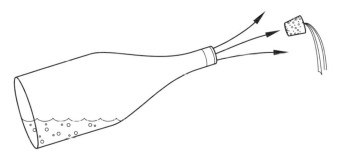

Vinegar and baking soda in a bottle produce carbon dioxide gas. The resulting pressure will expel a cork.

vinegar and baking soda produces carbon dioxide gas. If the
reaction is sluggish, shake the bottles slightly. (An alternative
to the vinegar and baking soda reaction is to put water in the
bottles and drop in chips of Alka Seltzer tablets.)

After the pressure builds up sufficiently, the corks will loudly
pop out and travel across the room. (Ribbon streamers may be
attached to the corks ahead of time.) When a particular cork
will actually be expelled is unpredictable, just like people's tem-
pers. Have a towel handy to catch the foam that often overflows
from the bottles.

Science Explanation

The chemicals involved in this demonstration are vinegar—
a dilute solution of acetic acid, CH_3CO_2H; baking soda—sodium
bicarbonate, $NaHCO_3$; carbon dioxide gas, CO_2. Carbon dioxide
forms in large amounts when vinegar and baking soda are combined. This harmless gas is also in carbonated drinks to give
them their "fizz." A container of pop when thoroughly shaken
and then opened gives an effect similar to that of this lesson's
demonstration.

12

Splash!

Theme: Those who trust in the Lord are secure.

Bible Verse: *Fear of man will prove to be a snare, but whoever trusts in the* LORD *is kept safe* (Prov. 29:25).

Materials Needed:
A bucket
Water

Bible Lesson

Christians are not immune to worry and doubt in this uncertain world. They do not have to face the problems of life in their own strength, however. Their lives are built on a strong foundation that cannot be shaken. Whatever happens, believers know that the Lord is present from the beginning to the end. Remembering the Lord's strength during times of trial will result in two benefits. First, Christians can testify of God's grace to others. Second, this can be a time of spiritual growth. Life may be difficult at times, but it is also exciting to see how the Lord helps believers through tough situations. Their success lies in knowing that God is in control.

Science Demonstration

This is an activity that many of us did as youngsters. The trick is to twirl a bucket of water in a vertical circle without spilling. If the bucket is moved faster than a certain minimum speed (about ten feet per second), the water cannot possibly spill out. At the top of the arc when the bucket is upside down, the downward gravity force simply causes the water to move in the circle rather than to spill downward. This busy life sometimes seems to "whirl" like the bucket, and we wonder if we have lost control. However, just as the water cannot escape the bucket, the Christian is entirely secure in the arms of the Lord.

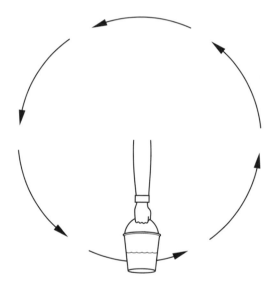

Water in a bucket that is swung swiftly in a vertical circle will not spill out.

Begin by showing everyone an empty bucket. It should have a secure handle that cannot come loose. Then pour about a quart of water into the bucket to show there is no trick. The amount of water does not matter; it does not affect the necessary bucket speed. After you pour water from a jar, you can also drop the jar into the bucket, just for good measure. Begin the circling motion with a few back-and-forth swings at the bottom of the arc. You will automatically feel how fast the bucket must move to safely revolve in a complete circle. You can then minimize the speed, slowing the bucket to the point where the water becomes slightly unstable at the top of the circle. This is also a good activity for a volunteer to perform. Make sure that there is adequate clearance on all sides for swinging.

Science Explanation

Circular motion is common in nature. Consider, for example, the moon's orbit around the earth. Like the spinning bucket the moon circles the earth with a constant speed of over two thousand miles per hour. And yet there is no danger of the moon escaping into the cold depths of space or of crashing into the earth. Instead, the moon remains within the firm grasp of the earth's gravity force.

Circular motion always requires an inward pull. This is called the centripetal force, which means "toward the center" of the circle. It may be gravity, a string pulling inward on a ball, or a strong arm holding a bucket.

God's strength may be invisible like gravity, but it is likewise dependable. After all, it is God who established gravity and the rules for circular motion.

13

Floating on Air

Theme: The Lord provides "wind beneath our wings," giving us support.

Bible Verse:
But those who hope in the LORD
will renew their strength.
They will soar on wings like eagles;
they will run and not grow weary,
they will walk and not be faint (Isa. 40:31).

Materials Needed:
Hair dryer
Balloon or lightweight ball

Bible Lesson

To hope in the Lord, or to wait upon the Lord, does not mean to give up or to sit back and do nothing. Instead it means not to give in to the pressures and temptations of life. It is to trust steadily in God, fully expecting him to make things right in the end.

Eagles can fly with no apparent effort. They will soar for hours on thermals—rising currents of warm air. Likewise, Christians have invisible support from on high. This is not to say that we will never get sick or experience failure. The promise is that God will be with us during the high times of soaring and also during the low times of testing. The promise involves exchanging a reliance on our own limited strength for complete trust in Christ. Lasting strength, freedom, and endurance come only from God.

Science Demonstration

Perhaps you have seen this demonstration in a store window as an eye-catcher. A ball is suspended permanently in the air by a vacuum hose. It jumps and bounces around but does not fall. In science this is called the Bernoulli effect, whereby the ball is supported by the stream of moving air. The air pressure is actually smaller within the airstream than it is around the outside. The greater outside pressure pushes inward on the ball from all sides, thus suspending it in the moving air. Whenever the ball begins to leave the airstream, higher pressure pushes it back into the center.

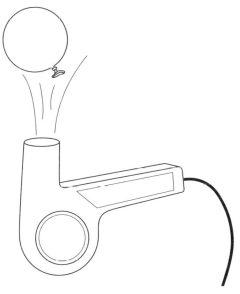

A balloon or lightweight ball placed in the airstream of a hair dryer will float in the air.

The electric hair dryer must have a good speed of air, which need not be heated. Hold the dryer steady or fasten it to a support. A balloon, light ball, some cotton, or even a paper wad can be supported by the upward airflow. A vacuum cleaner also works well, but only if the airflow can be reversed from suction to an outward airflow. With a more powerful blower, a fairly heavy object such as a screwdriver can be floated in the airstream.

Objects will remain suspended as long as the invisible airstream is active. Stop the airflow by covering the source with your hand, and the object will fall. In the same way, an eagle would fall from the sky if it lost its supporting air. For the believer, there is no such danger of a power failure.

Science Explanation

The change in pressure caused by moving air can be substantial. For example, an airplane wing is designed to cause greater air speed above the wing surface than below. This results in higher pressure beneath the wing than above. The many thousand of pounds of upward lift cause the plane to fly. Winged flight is not possible on the moon, where there is no air and therefore no pressure differences.

Daniel Bernoulli expressed the speed-pressure principle in 1738: "The pressure of a fluid decreases with increased velocity of the fluid." This Bernoulli effect is also responsible for such details as the curving of a baseball and the motion of a frisbee.

14

A Quick Change

Theme: Now is the time to trust in the Lord; later may be too late.

Bible Verses: *Two men will be in the field; one will be taken and the other left. Two women will be grinding with a hand mill; one will be taken and the other left* (Matt. 24:40–41).

Materials Needed:
Tablecloth or sheet of smooth material without a hem
Assorted tableware

Bible Lesson

This lesson is somewhat similar to lesson 20 concerning "the twinkling of an eye" from 1 Corinthians 15:51–52. In this day of self-sufficiency it is important to remember that the world is temporary and life is short. The Lord began this present world, and he will also end it someday. The Scripture lesson describes the second coming of Christ after the time of distress is past (Matt. 24:29). Two people working side-by-side will be separated, one to judgment while the other is left to enjoy the Lord's

presence. Verses 37–39 compare this separation to the great
flood, when the wicked perished and the faithful remained safe
on board the ark. The message still applies to us. We should
always be prepared and ready for the Lord's coming.

Science Demonstration

This demonstration is quick and dramatic. It involves a small
tablecloth (without a hem), dishes, a glass, and silverware. Use
a small table covering, about four feet by four feet, and dishes
that are somewhat heavy (and inexpensive). For added effect, fill
the glass with water. When preparations are complete, take hold
of an edge of the table covering with both hands. Add to the
suspense by acting unsure of yourself. Pull it slowly to show
that everything moves. Then quickly jerk the tablecloth off the
table in a downward direction. The place setting should be left
undisturbed. If a napkin is placed on the dish, it too will be
undisturbed. Practice this activity ahead of time, as always.

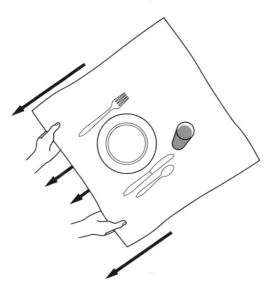

When a tablecloth is pulled away quickly, the place setting is left undisturbed.

The table items are said to have inertia. The rapid motion of the tablecloth does not put any appreciable force on the items, and they are left behind on the table. Suddenly, the objects are no longer setting on the tablecloth; their surroundings have been completely changed. Similarly, life conditions at any moment can change very quickly, especially when the Lord returns.

Science Explanation

The law of inertia was studied by Galileo and Isaac Newton. It states that objects at rest remain at rest, and objects in motion remain in motion, unless a force is applied.

The root meaning of the word *inertia* is "lazy" or "sluggish." All objects, including tableware, have inertia. Thus they resist sudden motion, such as a pulled tablecloth, since the force is not directly placed on the objects.

15

Tornado in a Bottle

Theme: We should turn our lives over to the one who is in charge of his creation.

Bible Verse: *He got up, rebuked the wind and said to the waves, "Quiet! Be still!" Then the wind died down and it was completely calm* (Mark 4:39).

Materials Needed:
  Two 2-liter clear plastic pop bottles
  Short section of tubing or hose
  Water
  Bits of paper or plastic

Bible Lesson

The Sea of Galilee is well known for its sudden storms. Strong winds often descend from the surrounding hills and violently stir up the waves. One day Jesus and the disciples were crossing the sea. While Jesus slept, a storm arose which threatened to sink the boat and drown them all. When Jesus was awakened, he quickly calmed the wind and waves by his word alone. Even more quickly than it arrived the storm disappeared.

The disciples were amazed at the Lord's obvious power over nature. This is the same Lord whom we are invited to love and serve today. "Salvation is found in no one else, for there is no other name under heaven given to men by which we must be saved" (Acts 4:12).

Science Demonstration

Fill one clear, two-liter pop bottle about three-quarters full with water. Connect a similar bottle to it so that it is somewhat in the shape of an hourglass. A threaded coupling can sometimes be purchased in gift shops for this purpose; a two-inch section of large tubing or garden hose will also work. The commercial connector usually has a small, three-eighths inch con-

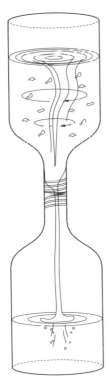

A "minitornado" can be formed inside two plastic bottles as water swirls between them.

striction, which extends the time it takes for the water to move
from one bottle to the other. This can also be accomplished by
leaving one bottle cap on, with a hole punched in the cap. For
one-time use, the two bottles can be connected with masking
tape wrapping their openings together.

When the bottles are inverted, and the upper one is moved
rapidly in a small circle, a tornado-like swirling begins as the
water pours through the neck to the lower bottle. The empty-
ing process takes about thirty seconds and is fascinating to
watch. Some small paper or plastic confetti added to the water
will enhance the visual effect.

Once the whirlpool begins, it becomes quite vigorous and
uncontrolled. The swirling action will continue until the water
completely drains to the lower bottle. This small "storm" cannot
be stopped, even though it is confined to a plastic bottle. Contrast this with the dangerous storm on the Sea of Galilee, which
Christ stopped instantly.

Science Explanation

The water passing between the bottles undergoes turbulent
motion. In science this term describes the complicated swirling
motion of liquids or gases. It occurs in ocean currents, clouds,
and within various pipelines. Turbulence is not well understood
scientifically. The shape and motion of the whirlpool within the
bottles cannot be predicted. That is, equations are not available
to exactly describe the motion. Turbulence is one of the great
unsolved problems of physics.

It sometimes appears that science has all the answers, and
scientific findings are often presented with dogmatism and
aloofness. In truth, every scientific discovery gives rise to mul-
tiple new and unanswered questions. And some areas, such as
turbulence, may simply remain beyond understanding. However, the Creator has complete knowledge and control of nature,
whether of the mighty ocean currents or a "tornado" within a
bottle.

16

An Empty Heart

Theme: Our lives are controlled either by good or by evil forces; the choice is ours.

Bible Verse: *When an evil spirit comes out of a man, it goes through arid places seeking rest and does not find it. Then it says, "I will return to the house I left"* (Luke 11:24).

Materials Needed:
A jar
A boiled, shelled egg
Section of newspaper
Lighter or matches
(Perhaps better done on a noncarpeted area)

Bible Lesson

In Luke 11:24–26 (and also Matt. 12:43–45) Jesus describes a man who has been freed from an evil spirit. Although his life is swept clean, this man does not replace the former evil with the new presence of the Holy Spirit. Instead his heart is left empty and vulnerable to reinvasion. The evil spirit then returns with seven others, and soon the man is worse off than he was before. When God's Spirit does not reside within a person, evil will surely fill the vacuum. It does no good to attempt to clean up one's life if the evil is not replaced with good. In fact, as Scripture shows, the situation may grow worse. We must fill our hearts and minds with the things of the Lord so that he may have control.

Science Demonstration

This demonstration is dramatic and fun. Obtain an empty glass jar (fruit juice, for example) with an opening somewhat smaller than a shelled, hard-boiled egg. The jar represents a person's heart, and the egg represents an evil spirit. Air will be removed from the jar to "sweep it clean." As a result, the egg will then be sucked into the empty jar.

First, show the group that the egg is too large to be pushed inside the jar. Then light one end of a rolled-up piece of paper,

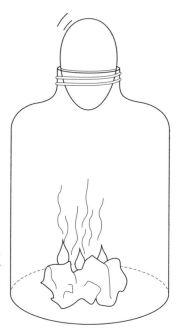

A hard-boiled egg placed over the opening of a jar with burning paper inside will be pushed into the jar.

perhaps a 10" x 10" piece of newspaper. When the paper is burning well, quickly and carefully drop it down inside the jar and set the egg on top, smaller end pointed downward. At first hot air will be expelled from the jar and the egg will vibrate. You may have to steady the egg at this time so it doesn't jump completely off the top. Within seconds, however, the air will be consumed inside the jar and the flame will go out. The remaining gas will cool and contract, resulting in a smaller inside air pressure. At this point, the greater outside air pressure will quickly push the egg down inside the jar with a loud burping sound. You might comment on how evil similarly returns to enter an empty heart. If the jar top is available, replace it to keep the resulting smoke smell from entering the room.

The egg can also be removed from the jar. First, hold the jar upside down and shake it until the egg covers the opening. You may have to withdraw the burned paper or push it out of the way. Still holding the bottle upside down, give a sharp upward blow of air into it. The air should move past the egg, increasing the inside air pressure and sending the egg flying back out of the jar. Move quickly out of the way after blowing in the jar, or you may get hit by the egg. Explain that evil (the egg) must be replaced by God's presence (the breath of air).

Science Explanation

The egg-in-the-bottle demonstration is often misunderstood. It is commonly thought that the flame uses up all the air inside the jar, leading to a vacuum. However, this is not the case. In the burning process, oxygen combines with carbon to form carbon dioxide gas, CO_2, which is not a vacuum.

Actually, heat is responsible for the vacuum effect. When the inside air is heated, its volume increases two or more times. This increase readily escapes from the jar around the sides of the egg. The egg serves as a flexible, one-way valve that lets air out of the jar but not back in. Then, when the flame is extinguished, the inside air quickly cools and contracts. Outside air then pushes the egg into the resulting partial vacuum within the jar.

17

A Special Friendship

Theme: Christians should give special help and encouragement to each other.

Bible Verse: *All men will know that you are my disciples, if you love one another* (John 13:35).

Materials Needed:
Strings, weights to make pendulums
Supports to suspend them

Bible Lesson

Love is an identifying characteristic of Christians. This is not a mushy, sentimental love, but a deep concern for the welfare of others. It is the opposite of selfishness. We are told to love our neighbors, which means everyone we come in contact with (Matt. 22:39). John 13:35 describes a special love between believers. This mutual care within the family of God should be clearly visible to the world.

In our day there are many public examples of arguments and lawsuits, between Christians and non-Christians alike. People have become skeptical of real love for lack of examples; selfishness is everywhere. More than ever before, the beautiful testimony of Christian love is needed. It is a bright, guiding light that can attract others to Christ.

Science Demonstration

Tie several pendulums to a slack horizontal supporting string, which should be attached to the backs of two chairs placed about four feet apart. Each pendulum has a different length, with just two of them being equal. Lengths between two and three feet will work well. (It is not critical that the pendulums have exactly the same weights suspended on them.) One suggestion is to use marbles taped to the strings. When one of the equal pendulums is started swinging, the others will vibrate somewhat. However, the matching pendulum will gradually pick up motion, and finally the two will swing together. If the described motion does not occur, try tightening the top supporting string. If the matched pendulums are not quite equal in length, something else interesting happens: The first pendulum will cease moving altogether, giving all its energy to its partner. Then the process will reverse itself and the original pendulum will slowly regain its motion. The two equal-length pendulums are in resonance, or in tune, with each other.

Christians should support and energize each other as do the two matched pendulums. There is a special bond or connection

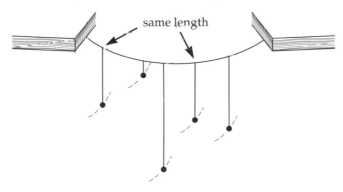

When several pendulums suspended from a slack string are put into motion, the two with equal lengths will swing together.

between them. Other people (the remaining pendulums) are not ignored, but there is an obvious link between the true believers. Just as the two equal pendulums energize each other and share their motion, Christians share the love of Christ and also extend it to others.

Science Explanation

Matched pendulums are said to be in resonance with each other. Since they have the same length and period, they can freely exchange their identical swinging motion. This is not possible for pendulums that are not "in tune" with each other.

There are many related examples of resonance. If a swing is continually pushed in synchronism with its motion, the child will soon be swinging through a high arc (see demonstration 28). Also, some cars have a particular speed at which an uncomfortable vibration is felt. There is apparently a resonance coupling between the car's motion on the highway and the car springs. At other speeds below and above this particular value, less vibration is noticed.

18

Walking through Doors

Theme: God is not limited by space and location as we are.

Bible Verse: *On the evening of that first day of the week, when the disciples were together, with the doors locked for fear of the Jews, Jesus came and stood among them and said, "Peace be with you!"* (John 20:19).

Materials Needed:
A sheet of paper 8 1/2" x 11" or smaller
Scissors

Bible Lesson

It is clear from the Bible verse that Jesus could pass through closed, locked doors. This was not a mere trick or magic. Jesus' physical body was changed following his resurrection, and he could appear and disappear whenever he wanted. Similar examples are found in John 20:26 and Luke 24. The lesson is clear that Jesus was much more than a man. He was also the Son of God and had supernatural abilities. Jesus is all that he claimed to be; there is no one else equal to him. That is why he deserves all of our attention and praise.

Another lesson is that the Lord is with the believer, wherever that person is. You cannot hide from God, and you are also never beyond his help. This should motivate Christians to live righteously and comfort them in times of trouble. Suppose you were lost in the woods, or locked behind bars, or even exploring deep space. As a Christian, you can be certain that the Lord would also be present; he is never lost or locked out.

Science Demonstration

Hold up a sheet of paper and tell your audience that you are going to walk through it. The very idea sounds strange and impossible, but it can be done easily. While you talk, perhaps

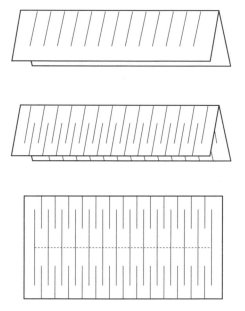

Fold a sheet of paper lengthwise and make overlapping, inward cuts. Open the sheet, cut down the center, and open into a large loop.

describing the background of the Bible verse, fold and cut a sheet of paper as shown.

Fold the paper in half, lengthwise. Cut slits from the fold, stopping just short of the edges. Now make cuts from the edges toward the fold, between the first cuts, stopping just short of the fold. The narrower the slits, the better. The cuts are shown in the figure as straight lines. Now open the sheet and cut along the fold, from the first to the last cut (dotted line). Carefully open up the sheet to reveal a large circular ribbon of paper, which you can easily step or walk through. Practice the cutting process beforehand with scrap paper. If the slits are made close to each other, this trick can even be done with a small index card.

"Walking through paper," of course, is far more artificial than Jesus' ability to pass through closed doors. As with the other activities in this book, the goal is simply to turn our eyes and thoughts to the truth of Scripture. Someday, when believers have glorified bodies, then perhaps they too will be able to walk right through closed doors. The future is indeed exciting for Christians.

Science Explanation

Suppose an 8 1/2" x 11" sheet of paper is cut as illustrated with one-quarter-inch strips. When opened up, the ring of paper will be fourteen feet around. This is nearly the size of a doorway. A smaller sheet of paper will result in a smaller opening, but one that will still be large enough to slip over your head and shoulders.

You may have heard it said that matter is mostly empty space. Individual atoms indeed have most of their mass concentrated in the center nucleus. Electrons orbit this nucleus, somewhat similar to planets orbiting the sun. If a scale model is made of an atom, with the nucleus made the size of a baseball, then the electrons will be at an outer distance of six miles. That is, electrons are very small and comparatively far distant from the nucleus. Thus it is true that atoms are mostly empty space.

Some have suggested that the emptiness of matter was somehow rearranged to allow the Lord to walk through closed doors. This may be true, but we must resist the effort to explain the details of miracles. The Lord has supreme power over the physical universe. The ways of the Lord are beyond our finite understanding (Rom. 11:33).

19

A Mystery

Theme: Someday the Lord will increase our understanding.

Bible Verse: *Now we see but a poor reflection as in a mirror; then we shall see face to face. Now I know in part; then I shall know fully, even as I am fully known* (1 Cor. 13:12).

Materials Needed:
Two index cards
Scissors
Glue stick or paper clips

Bible Lesson

On this side of heaven the Christian does not have simple answers to many difficult questions, such as:

How did God create the universe from nothing?
How can God be three persons in one?
Why is there suffering in the world?
Why does Jesus love me?

We cannot expect to completely understand these deep truths. Only God has full understanding, and his ways are past finding out (Rom. 11:33). It is like seeing an unclear image in a mirror. The picture is there, but the details are blurry. At a future time all the unsolved mysteries of life will be made clear. From the vantage point of heaven, our questions will quickly disappear. This truth should be a comfort to the believer during troubling times. Someday we will better understand God's purpose in events. We will realize how he answered our prayers in the best possible, loving way. Meanwhile, life's mysteries provide opportunities to exercise our faith in God.

Science Demonstration

This activity works best with a smaller group. You will appear to cut and fold a card in an impossible way. Of course it only looks impossible; the trick is simple when you explain it.

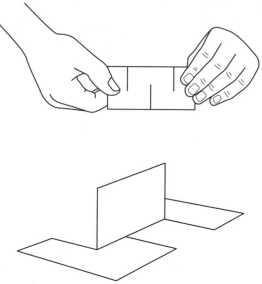

An unusual sculpture results from cutting the card along the inside lines and folding as instructed.

Cut three slits in a card, as shown by the lines. Now hold the card level with the double slit facing you. Place your right thumb on top of the card and your left thumb beneath. Rotate your left hand and twist the card and fold it so it looks like the lower diagram. Do this quickly. Now glue or paper clip the strange-looking sculpture to another card and pass it around for inspection. The glue or paper clip prevents your audience from quickly discovering the trick. Just as the events of life are not always clear, the paper sculpture looks impossible to make.

Take your sculpture apart, or make another one to show the technique. If time permits, you might let group members construct the sculpture for themselves. This way they will better remember the demonstration as well as the Scripture application of understanding a mystery.

Science Explanation

The paper sculpture is simply an optical illusion. The deceptive appearance of the folded card makes it look impossible. Upon closer inspection, however, every optical illusion has a commonsense explanation.

This paper-folding exercise actually relates to the branch of mathematics called topology. It includes the nature and transformation of surfaces and areas. They can be expressed mathematically as well as actually be constructed. There are a large number of interesting paper-cutting-and-folding exercises that can be explored.

20

The Twinkling of an Eye

Theme: At the Lord's command in the end time, all believers on earth will be instantly changed, whether they are dead or alive.

Bible Verses: *Listen, I tell you a mystery: We will not all sleep, but we will all be changed—in a flash, in the twinkling of an eye, at the last trumpet. For the trumpet will sound, the dead will be raised imperishable, and we will be changed* (1 Cor. 15:51–52).

Materials Needed: Rulers (one for every two people)

Bible Lesson

The Lord is very patient with the human race. Nearly two thousand years have passed since Christ physically left the earth and ascended into heaven. However, at his command end-time events could begin on planet Earth. He has power over time and also over death. The above Scripture passage describes events at the conclusion of this age. The bodies of those believers who have died (are asleep) will be resurrected. Believers who are alive likewise will be instantly changed. Physical death will give way to victory and eternal life through our Lord Jesus Christ (1 Cor. 15:57).

The event is described as happening in a moment or flash of time. The Greek word used here gives us the modern word *atom,* meaning small and indivisible. The twinkling or briefest movement of an eye describes the supernatural change of the Lord's children. This Scripture promise is a comfort during trials. Someday the Lord will return and make things right. We can rejoice in God's power over nature and look forward to the time when we are changed to be more like him.

For the unbeliever there is no promise of additional time to make a decision for the Lord. There is no assurance of health or life itself from one moment to the next. In a flash the opportunity for salvation could be lost forever. "Now is the day of salvation" (2 Cor. 6:2).

Science Demonstration

This activity will make us more aware of a brief instant of time. It is a simple technique to measure a person's reaction time, usually a fraction of a second. The person must catch a ruler between his or her separated fingers after it is released by another person. The marks on the ruler show how many inches

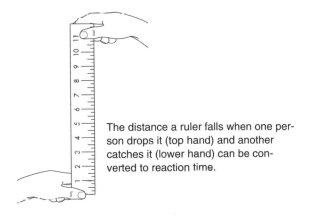

The distance a ruler falls when one person drops it (top hand) and another catches it (lower hand) can be converted to reaction time.

the ruler falls before the fingers actually pinch closed and stop the falling ruler. Measure the length that has fallen below the fingers. The following table converts inches of fall into approximate time. The table can be written on a chalkboard or overhead projector.

Fall of ruler (inches)	Time (seconds)
2	.10
4	.14
6	.18
8	.20
10	.23
12	.25

This measurement is fun to make and averages about six inches for most people, a reaction time of .18 second. Because of this built-in reaction delay, a person cannot catch a dollar bill that is held by someone else halfway down between his or her fingers and then dropped. The half-length of a dollar bill is just three inches, too short for our typical reaction time. Stress the illustration of an instant of time, the mere twinkling of an eye when the ruler falls. The Lord is able to do mighty works on this short time scale.

Science Explanation

At the earth's surface, objects fall because of the downward pull of the earth's gravity. Disregarding air resistance, free fall does not depend upon the weight of the object. That is, light and heavy rulers will fall with identical motion.

For any free-fall distance *(d)*, the falling time *(t)* can be calculated from the relation

$$t = \sqrt{\frac{2d}{g}}$$

where *g* is the acceleration due to gravity,

$$g = 32 \text{ feet/second}^2$$
$$= 384 \text{ inches/second}^2$$

On a larger scale, the formula gives the following times for
longer distances:

Fall distance (feet)	Time (seconds)
16	1
32	2
64	3
256	4

On the moon, where gravity is less, objects fall more slowly,
somewhat as in slow motion. On Jupiter gravity is nearly
three times greater than on earth. There a dropped ruler
would rapidly shoot downward.

21

Safe from Blows

Theme: The Lord provides full protection from attacks by Satan.

Bible Verse: *Put on the full armor of God so that you can take your stand against the devil's schemes* (Eph. 6:11).

Materials Needed:
    Heavy pine board or a two-by-four, about 1 foot long
    Hammer and nails
    Bible or large book
    A volunteer

Bible Lesson

In Ephesians 6:10–20, the Christian's life is described as an ongoing warfare. The enemy is Satan (and his fallen-angel followers). However, the believer has an overwhelming array of weapons that will defeat any foe. These pieces of invincible armor include truth (v. 14), righteousness (v. 14), the gospel of peace (v. 15), faith (v. 16), salvation (v. 17), the Bible (v. 17), and prayer (v. 18). The effective use of these weapons requires lifelong training in discipleship, Bible study, ministry, and outreach. The final outcome of this battle between the forces of good and evil is already determined. All Christians are on the winning side.

Satanic symbols and the occult are popular in the world today. Many foolish people, both young and old, are captivated by this unhealthy activity. Certainly these evil practices should not be touched by believers. At the same time, however, we need not have unreasonable fear or worry about the dark side of the spirit world. We have heavenly armor available, which leaves the devil powerless to defeat us.

Science Demonstration

You are the "victim" in this activity. Sit on a chair, holding a book and also a board on top of your head. Have someone drive a nail into the board on your head. It is noisy, but it should not hurt. Almost all the hammer's energy goes into the moving nail. Have the volunteer stop before the nail is completely seated, or the hammering may become uncomfortable. A soft cover on the book is helpful, since it will spread the impact over a larger area.

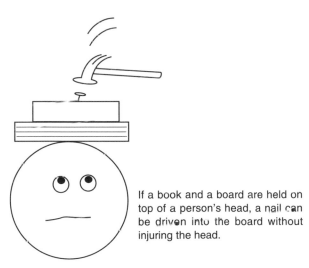

If a book and a board are held on top of a person's head, a nail can be driven into the board without injuring the head.

The larger the book and board, the better, since their inertia will help protect what is underneath, namely your head.

One suggestion for a book is the Bible. With this choice you must be careful that the Bible is not looked upon as a gimmick. With this caution in mind, the activity becomes a graphic illustration of the power of the Word to protect us from attack by the evil one. You might conclude by explaining that Ephesians does not describe literal armor such as a helmet (v. 17). Instead, the armor is from God and can never rust or be pierced.

Science Explanation

Lesson 14 introduced the concept of inertia. This describes the natural resistance of objects to any rapid change of motion. More massive objects have more inertia and thus more resistance to change.

When the nail is hit sharply, it absorbs most of the hammer's energy. The supporting board and book move very little because of their combined inertia. The book is also in contact with a large area of the top of the head, which further spreads out any resulting force.

Professionals perform this demonstration by holding a brick against their chest while a helper hits it with a sledge hammer. The brick can be crumbled with no injury to the performer.

22

A Dependable Universe

Theme: God continually watches over his universe and keeps it operating through his physical laws.

Bible Verse: *[God is] sustaining all things by his powerful word* (Heb. 1:3).

Materials Needed:
A tennis ball, or similar-size ball
Five-foot length of string

Bible Lesson

It sometimes appears that this universe operates by itself. Clouds drift by, the moon circles the earth, and the planets orbit the sun. This orderly motion is maintained by the law of gravitation, discovered by Sir Isaac Newton three centuries ago. Gravity is an invisible force that causes objects to attract and hold on to each other. For example, the attractive force between the earth and moon causes the tides and also keeps the moon from escaping the earth. We can measure and calculate exactly the strength of gravity, but unsolved mysteries remain. Gravity is completely invisible, yet it is somehow able to act across millions of miles of empty space. Gravity never turns off or varies in any way whatsoever. Just try to defy gravity by stepping into the air.

Gravity also cannot be canceled out or shielded; it is always active. Furthermore, there is no reason why gravity should continue to exist entirely on its own. Clearly, this essential gravity "glue" that holds the universe together was established by the Creator. God also continually upholds this law of nature, just as he does all other parts of his creation. If God would turn his back on the universe for just one instant, chaos would immediately result everywhere. Life for us would end instantly. Without the laws of stability, planets and stars would all disintegrate. Shouldn't we put all our trust in the one who created and operates the universe?

Science Demonstration

Attach the string to the ball with a knot or tape so that it can be swung in a vertical circle, like a large wheel. The ball represents the orbiting earth, with your hand as the sun at the center of the circle. Ask your audience what will happen when you

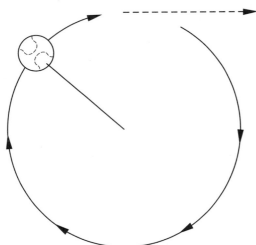

When a ball on a string is swung in a circle and released, it will leave on a straight-line tangent.

release the string at the top of the ball's arc. Will it go straight up and hit the ceiling, or come down and hit you? Try it and see, being careful of the target off to the side. The motion is similar to that of a stone leaving a sling. The ball will travel on a tangent, in roughly a straight-line direction. This is exactly what the earth would do if gravity suddenly ceased to exist. Our planet would leave the sun behind, and life for us would quickly grow cold, dark, and impossible. There would also be major trouble on earth itself if its gravity turned off. Anything not fastened down, including water, pets, people, even air, would float into space.

Fortunately, God holds his laws of the universe constant.

Gravity is a continual reminder of God's faithfulness: "I will declare that your love stands firm forever, that you established your faithfulness in heaven itself" (Ps. 89:2).

Science Explanation

When the ball is released during its swing, it does not travel on exactly a straight path. Instead, the earth's gravity attraction pulls downward on the ball. As the ball moves horizontally, it follows a parabolic path to the ground. The curvature of this motion is slight enough that it does not interfere with the demonstration.

Gravity remains a mysterious force in nature. It acts through great distances of empty space. The gravitational attraction between the earth and sun also continually adjusts to the earth's changing location. There is scientific speculation that invisible gravity particles called gravitons, or perhaps gravity waves, continually flow between space objects like the earth and sun. However, these particles or waves have not yet been detected. We are reminded of Colossians 1:17, which states that God holds all things together, including the moon, earth, sun, and stars.

23

Piercing the Heart

Theme: God's Word shows our need and gives us hope.

Bible Verse: *For the word of God is living and active. Sharper than any double-edged sword, it penetrates even to dividing soul and spirit, joints and marrow; it judges the thoughts and attitudes of the heart* (Heb. 4:12).

Materials Needed:
  Two balloons, a light-colored large one and a dark-colored small one
  A large pin or needle

Bible Lesson

For the Christian, the Bible is a special book. It is God's written word. We read about the creation of humankind and about their past successes and failures. Happily we also read about Christ's love for us and his remedy for our sin. As we study the Bible it should cause us to take action. God's Word discloses our inward thoughts and challenges our hearts to faith and upright living. What will we do with this invitation?

Science Demonstration

The outer balloon should be large, ten or more inches in diameter, and light colored so it is somewhat transparent. The inner balloon should be smaller and dark colored for visibility. Insert the small balloon into the large one by pushing it inward with the eraser end of a pencil. Then blow up the inner balloon completely and knot the end. Now inflate the outer balloon, but not fully, and knot it also. The inner balloon should bounce around freely inside.

When it is time for the activity, grasp the large balloon and squeeze it so that the inner balloon is forced up against the top near the nozzle. The underinflated outer balloon will have some

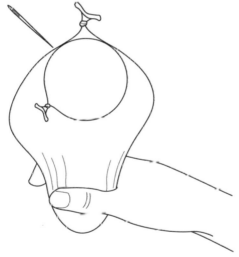

A small, completely inflated balloon inside a large, partially inflated balloon can be popped with a pin from the outside.

flexible "give" around the top, whereas the inner balloon has a relatively hard surface. If a pin is now slowly pressed deeply against the top of the outer balloon, it will make an indentation without actual puncture. However, the inner balloon should loudly pop. Usually the outer balloon is unharmed; sometimes

an unnoticed pinhole is formed. Shake the large balloon to show
the fragments from the inner balloon within.

The inner balloon represents our inner being. It is hidden by
outer appearance (the large balloon). The Lord is not stopped
by outside barriers. His Word enters our hearts and probes like
the pin that pricks the inner balloon. When we come to know
the Lord, the real change takes place on the inside of our lives.
The transition from an inflated balloon to small pieces shows
how complete and dramatic this change is.

Science Explanation

A pin-prick hole in a balloon becomes a sudden point of
weakness. A tear begins and quickly moves across the surface of
the balloon with a pop. In engineering terms, this is called pro-
gressive failure of the balloon skin.

In this demonstration, the outer balloon is protected by hav-
ing a flexible, underinflated skin. It deflects greatly without tearing. Another way to protect the outer balloon is to put a piece of
transparent Scotch tape on its surface. A needle can then be
inserted directly through the tape without destroying the balloon; only a small leak will result.

24

Nothing Hidden

Theme: God clearly knows whether or not we belong to him.

Bible Verse: *Nothing in all creation is hidden from God's sight. Everything is uncovered and laid bare before the eyes of him to whom we must give account* (Heb. 4:13).

Materials Needed:
Two glass jars or test tubes
Liquid dishwashing detergent
Hard water and soft water samples

Bible Lesson

Hebrews 4:12–13 explains that God's Word is powerful. It is a judge of our actions and innermost thoughts. Our standing before God may be evaluated by the standard of Scripture. Verse 13 declares that it is impossible to keep any secrets from God. We may fool others and even ourselves with hidden motives, but everything is on open display before God. He knows who is telling the truth and who is on his side. This is a sober warning but also a comforting thought. God knows what is true and false in this world. He also understands our innermost hurts and fears. In fact, he knows us better than we know ourselves.

Science Demonstration

This lesson makes visible something that is usually unseen. The example given here is both easy and familiar. Two kinds of water are needed: hard and soft. In many places ground water is naturally hard because of dissolved calcium, magnesium, or iron. Because these atoms are in solution, they are invisible to the eye. Bottled mineral water will also suffice. Softened water is available in many homes. Rain or distilled water can also be used for soft water. The two types of water, hard and soft, look identical. We cannot easily tell them apart, although there is a large internal difference. Likewise, people may be similar in outward appearance. We cannot see within the heart to determine what a person really stands for, but God can.

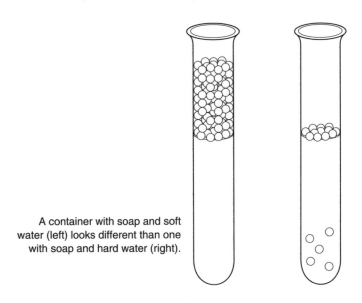

A container with soap and soft water (left) looks different than one with soap and hard water (right).

Put the two water types into separate jars or test tubes, about half full. (So that a large audience can see the demonstration, use two-liter plastic soft drink bottles.) Add a few drops of dish-washing detergent to each container. Now, with the tops sealed, simultaneously shake the two containers equally for about thirty seconds. The difference between the two water types should now be obvious:

Soft water	Hard water
Lots of suds on top	Has a "bathtub ring"
Soap is dissolved	Little suds
Water quickly clears	Soap left over
Looks clean	Water is milky

The impurities in the hard water prevent the soap from per-forming properly. Instead, a messy white precipitate forms, sometimes known as bathtub ring. The pinch of soap dramati-cally reveals the difference in the water types. Our inner, hidden thoughts are just as open and apparent before God's eyes.

Science Explanation

If samples of hard and soft water are left out in the open to evaporate for a couple days, the difference becomes obvious. White scale material forms around the sides of the evaporating hard water. This white residue consists of calcium, magnesium, or iron. It is actually dissolved rock powder that precipitates with the loss of water.

The use of hard water may lead to a number of difficulties. The soap-hardness precipitate may leave a gummy residue behind during hair washing. In cooking, hard water will make food taste slightly "tough." Over time, hardness scale may com-pletely plug hot-water pipes. This extended lesson application shows the difficulties that develop and grow when problems are not dealt with.

25

What Is Faith?

Theme: Deep theological discussion of faith is interesting, but the simple faith of a child is completely effective for knowing God.

Bible Verse: *Now faith is being sure of what we hope for and certain of what we do not see* (Heb. 11:1).

Materials Needed:
   A banana
   Needle and thread

Bible Lesson

Many unbelievers are unfamiliar with the concept of faith. In this skeptical age, people claim not to trust in anything or in anyone beyond themselves. In contrast, the very word *faith* means belief or trust, especially in God. Hebrews 11, the great faith chapter, illustrates the concept.

What is faith? First, it is being sure. Faith results in complete confidence in the object of one's trust (v. 1). Second, faith is the key to understanding the creation of the universe (v. 3). Miracles such as creation cannot be comprehended, but they can be believed and appreciated. Third, faith is not an easy shortcut for unthinking people. Hebrews 11 is a roll call of honor for early believers who bravely displayed outstanding faith in difficult circumstances.

Faith in Christ is both the condition of salvation and one of its results. That is, through Christian growth and Bible study, faith will become ever deeper and richer. Faith is a great blessing of the Christian life. Let us give thanks for this precious gift.

Science Demonstration

No study could ever plumb the depths of Christian faith. This particular activity challenges the listeners in just one area, that of believing something they cannot see and which is, in fact, doubtful to them. Hold up a banana and ask if anyone could possibly believe that it is completely sliced, even though it has not been peeled. Real faith involves the action of stepping out and making a commitment; are there any volunteers? Of course, the idea sounds impossible. Who has ever seen an unpeeled banana already sliced? However, faith sometimes involves seemingly impossible events such as creation, miracles, and the resurrection. Continue an open discussion concerning the banana and faith:

Perhaps genetic presliced bananas have been developed.
Has anyone ever peeled a banana and found it already sliced?
If people want to inspect the banana, let them.
Tell them it *is* sliced, and see if anyone will believe you.

Finally, peel the banana and show that it is indeed presliced. Sometimes, faith in things unseen is entirely appropriate.

It is only fair to tell the group how you did the "trick." There are two ways to preslice a banana. The quick method is to insert a long, thin needle straight into the banana along a ridge. Push the needle from side to side, slicing through the soft inside. By feeling the outside of the banana, you can tell when the needle is cutting completely through the inside without tearing the outer peeling. When the needle is finally pulled out, its puncture mark should not be noticeable. Repeat this process several more times along the ridge until the inner banana is completely sliced along its length. Keep the needle clean so you can eventually eat some slices before the group. Practice this procedure ahead of time and inspect the results by peeling the bananas.

The second slicing method is more ingenious but also takes a bit longer. This time a needle with strong thread is pushed through the banana just under the peel, along a flat surface seg-

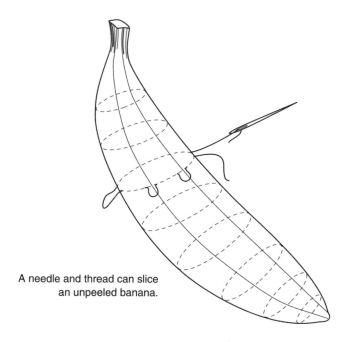

A needle and thread can slice
an unpeeled banana.

ment. Then the needle is reinserted into the next segment the same way, and on around the outside. The thread is finally drawn back out the original puncture hole. Finally, as the thread is pulled out it will slice through the banana. As before, this process is repeated several times along the banana's length. The result once again is a presliced, unpeeled banana.

Science Explanation

Genetic engineers are striving to produce new food items: square tomatoes for easier packaging and strawberries as large as apples. However, a presliced banana is not yet available. Besides a banana this demonstration can also be performed with an apple, slicing it from the "inside out" using a needle or straight pin.

26

Losing Excess Weight

Theme: We must be careful not to get involved with things that hinder our service to God.

Bible Verse: *Therefore, since we are surrounded by such a great cloud of witnesses, let us throw off everything that hinders and the sin that so easily entangles, and let us run the race marked out for us* (Heb. 12:1).

Materials Needed:

Swivel chair or turntable-type exerciser

Two heavy objects (books, weights, rocks, etc.)

Bible Lesson

The great cloud of witnesses in Hebrews 12:1 includes the group of heroes listed in chapter 11. These men and women gave the Lord first place in their lives. They were by no means perfect, but their faith helped them succeed in life. God likewise has a plan and purpose for each of us. We choose to fulfill this plan or frustrate it. Hebrews 12:1 reminds us to keep our eye on the goal of serving God with whatever talents and resources he has given to us.

A popular commercial has challenged the listener to be the best that he or she can be. In real life that goal is accomplished by heeding Hebrews 12:1 and giving God priority. This certainly does not mean that we must give up all our hobbies or recreation time. It does mean that we should consider how we spend our time and how involved we are with temporary, material things.

Science Demonstration

A swivel chair is needed, one that turns easily. An alternative could be a "trimmer exerciser," a turntable-type platform that a person stands on to exercise. Have a volunteer spin on the chair or platform. (If using a platform, you may want the volunteer to crouch or kneel to prevent him or her from falling.) Repeat this motion with the volunteer holding two weights with arms extended. While the person is freely turning he or she pulls the weights inward, close to the body. There will be a noticeable increased speed of the spinning motion. Motion can be

A person spins around on a swivel chair or disk, holding weights with arms extended. When the weights are drawn in toward the body the motion speeds up.

slowed again by extending the weights outward. It gives an interesting turning sensation, and others might like to try it afterward.

The turning effect involves the conservation of angular momentum. When rotating objects are drawn inward toward the center of motion, speed always increases as a result. We have all seen this done by figure skaters. The application is that just as extended weights slow us down, so the details of life can entangle us and hinder our service to God.

Science Explanation

Angular momentum (L) for a rotating object can be calculated from the relation $L = mwr$. The moving object's mass is m, angular speed w is in radians per second, and radial distance from the rotation axis is r. In the absence of any external torque on a rotating object, the object's angular momentum remains constant.

In the demonstration, the radial distance is decreased by pulling the weights inward. Then, since angular momentum and mass do not change, the angular speed increases and the person turns faster.

There are several basic conservation laws in nature, describing constant quantities: conservation of angular momentum, linear momentum, energy, and electric charge. Each of these quantities has been experimentally found exactly to obey laws of constancy. The existence of these important rules is a powerful testimony to the wisdom and planning of the Creator.

27

A Forest Fire

Theme: False rumors spread out of control in all directions.

Bible Verse: *Likewise the tongue is a small part of the body, but it makes great boasts. Consider what a great forest is set on fire by a small spark* (James 3:5).

Materials Needed:
Candle
Newspaper
Powder (talcum, cornstarch, or foot powder, for example)

Bible Lesson

Words can be used to build others up or to tear them down. Once a false statement is released, it has a life of its own and it spreads from person to person. It cannot be stopped or recalled; such efforts only fan the flame. James 3:3–4 compares the tongue to a horse's bridle, a ship's rudder, and a spark in a forest. Small items like the tongue can clearly have large consequences.

James 3:13 tells us to spread blessings instead of gossip: "Who is wise and understanding among you? Let him show it by his good life, by deeds done in the humility that comes from wisdom." Leviticus 19:16 also warns against false rumors: "Do not go about spreading slander among your people." The word for "slander" is elsewhere translated as "talebearing" or "gossip." Instead of acting against a neighbor, the Christian should "love your neighbor as yourself" (Lev. 19:18).

Science Demonstration

Like a rumor, a chain reaction continues and quickly spreads once it is started. There are many activities which illustrate a chain reaction, such as falling dominoes or one marble shot into a large group of marbles. The chain reaction described here is dramatic, and caution is needed. It involves a dust explosion.

Powder dropped into a flame will cause a chain
reaction.

When fine dust is suspended in the air, the dust can ignite and burn quickly. A spark can ignite one particle, which then burns surrounding dust. This is sometimes the cause of large explosions in grain elevators and dusty factories. Great effort must be made to avoid a spark in such places.

Light the candle, place it in a holder, and set it on a newspaper. The newspaper should be dampened slightly for fire safety. From a height of one to two feet above the candle, a large pinch of powder is dropped into the flame. It should ignite with a bright flame and a puff of smoke. I have found that certain fine powders work best: talcum powder, cornstarch, foot powder, etc. Flour will also readily burn if it is sifted first.

An alternative procedure is to build a simple apparatus that disperses the powder into the air. This can be done with a funnel, length of rubber tubing, and a squeeze bulb. Attach the bulb and the funnel to opposite ends of the tubing, and then place a tablespoon of the powder in the funnel. Aim the funnel just above the burning candle and squeeze the bulb. The powder should spray outward and burn brightly. This chain reaction illustrates how quickly a fire or a rumor can spread beyond control.

Science Explanation

Chain reactions often occur very quickly. When a single dust particle ignites, it produces smoke and flame as it vaporizes. This flame reaches several other suspended dust particles, which in turn continue the process with a substantial flash of combined heat.

Dust or powder settled on a surface usually will not burn. The particles must first be dispersed in the air. This surrounding air supply then helps the combustion process.

In a similar way, a solid piece of iron will not burn. However, if the iron is in the form of steel wool, with tiny fibers and plentiful air spaces, it will readily glow and burn.

Two other chain reactions are examples. First, dominoes can be set up in a fan-shaped arrangement so that the number that fall over progresses in the chain reaction series: one, two, four, eight, sixteen, thirty-two. . . . One falling domino triggers the entire cascade.

Second, a nuclear explosion is actually a runaway chain reaction. First, one uranium atom is split when a neutron particle collides with it. In the process, several more neutrons and also energy are released. The additional neutrons split other nearby uranium atoms, and an abundance of neutrons and energy is the instantaneous result. In a nuclear power plant, the uranium chain reaction is harnessed by limiting the number of available neutrons. Energy is then produced in a steady and safe manner.

28

Moving a Mountain

Theme: A faithful life, in prayer and in practice, brings results.

Bible Verse: *Confess your faults to each other and pray for each other so that you may be healed. The prayer of a righteous man is powerful and effective* (James 5:16).

Materials Needed:
   A heavy weight
   Strong cord
   Small hammer

Bible Lesson

James 5:16 reminds us that there is great power in prayer. Fervent prayer is steady, unhurried, and sincere. It is offered with full confidence of results. Using a prayer list illustrates fervent prayer. Items are prayed for on a daily basis, answered prayers are marked off as victories, and new items are added as they arise. If we only realized the true power of prayer, even (or especially) of that of a child, it would surely change our lives.

Science Demonstration

We will show how a small but steady effort can result in a major change. A heavy pendulum is needed—a weight such as a bucket of water or piece of metal suspended from the ceiling. A ceiling plant-hanger hook may support a pendulum. The cord should be carefully measured so that the total length from the top support to the center of the weight is thirty-nine inches. Any pendulum with this length will swing with a time period of exactly two seconds. The actual amount of the weight does not matter. If the weight is tapped once every two seconds by hand or a small hammer, it will slowly accumulate motion and soon be swinging widely. The process is similar to steadily pushing or pumping a swing to a high level.

With a little practice, you can easily tap the pendulum with the two-second rhythm. The many small taps will be gradually transferred into a much larger motion. Perhaps you will not move a mountain, but you will move something heavy. In a similar way, a consistent Christian life of prayer can lead to

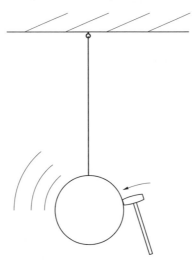

Tapping a large suspended object at regular inter-
vals with a small object results in the large object
swinging widely.

major results for God's glory. Success does not always only go to the swift and the strong but also to the faithful. Never underestimate the influence of a consistent Christian life.

This pendulum demonstration was once performed with a heavy suspended steel beam that was struck regularly by a small cork on a string. After ten minutes a slight vibration could be seen. After half an hour the entire beam swung like a mighty pendulum.

Your particular situation may require a different length of pendulum. The following table shows other lengths and corresponding time periods for one complete swing. One time period is a complete back-and-forth swing.

Length (inches)	Time (seconds)
10	1
39	2
61 (5 ft. 1 in.)	2.5
88 (7 ft. 4 in.)	3
156 (13 ft.)	4
243 (20 ft. 3 in.)	5

Science Explanation

Suppose a heavy pendulum is tapped by a small force of just one ounce, once each second. In one full minute the combined force will be almost four pounds. In five minutes the force will total almost nineteen pounds. In this way a small, steady push slowly increases in influence.

The list of pendulum lengths (l) and swinging periods (T) was calculated from the pendulum equation.

$$T = 2 \pi \sqrt{\frac{l}{g}}$$

Here π is the math constant 3.14 and g is the acceleration due to gravity (demonstration 20).

$$g = \quad 32 \ \text{feet/second}^2$$
$$= 384 \ \text{inches/second}^2$$

It is interesting that the period of a pendulum depends on the length but not on the size of the suspended weight.

29

A Perfect Balance

Theme: Don't be knocked off balance by false teachers.

Bible Verse: *Therefore, dear friends, since you already know this, be on your guard so that you may not be carried away by the error of lawless men and fall from your secure position* (2 Peter 3:17).

Materials Needed:
  Drinking glass
  Large kitchen utensil such as a ladle

Bible Lesson

There are many false teachers in the world today. Jude 13 calls them "wandering stars," those who do not provide a good example or proper direction. The believer must be on guard so that he or she is not misled by those who do not truly represent the Lord. In our day they may be found everywhere: in churches, on television, and in books. False teachers can be a great hindrance to faithful servants who are truly serving God.

By their misdirection such teachers keep others from receiving the gospel. They may also cause believers to lose their balance and their testimony. The best way to detect error is to thoroughly know God and his Word. A positive example is provided in Acts 17:11: The Bereans examined the Scriptures daily to see whether or not the messages they heard were true.

Science Demonstration

There are several ways to show balance. One way is to balance a large kitchen utensil on the edge of a drinking glass. Place a soup ladle upside down on the edge of a glass. When balanced, the ladle will easily rock back and forth but will not fall. With some practice you can also pour water from the glass without disturbing the balance of the ladle.

The suspended utensil can be said to represent the mature Christian life. Mature Christians are not easily led astray or knocked off balance. Instead, when swayed by temptation or trial their lives quickly return to a stable upright position before God.

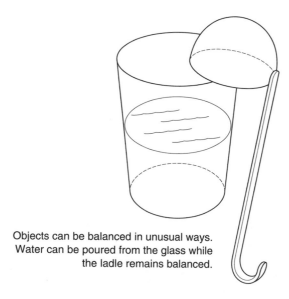

Objects can be balanced in unusual ways.
Water can be poured from the glass while
the ladle remains balanced.

Science Explanation

For an object to balance as shown in the drawing, its center of gravity or balance point must be directly beneath the top point of support. This will be true for a soup ladle if the handle is heavier than the cup portion.

With a low center of gravity, the weight of the object pulls straight down on the edge of the glass, providing a secure balance. Other utensils, such as a strainer, can be similarly balanced if they have a right-angle portion as does the ladle. On a strainer, a toothpick can also be pushed through a small opening to provide the right angle to be balanced on the glass.

30

Water of Life

Theme: Water is a precious natural resource. How much greater is the gift of salvation!

Bible Verse: *Whoever is thirsty, let him come; and whoever wishes, let him take the free gift of the water of life* (Rev. 22:17).

Materials Needed:
Two inflated balloons, one with water inside
Candle and lighter

Bible Lesson

Water is the natural resource most often mentioned in Scripture. In biblical times, people living among the dry hills of Palestine knew how precious water was. In Scripture water symbolizes the Holy Spirit and also the new birth (John 7:38–39). Consider some of the parallels between water and salvation:

Both are priceless yet free.
Both are available to all.
Water is essential for physical life; salvation for eternal life.

Although the gift of salvation goes far beyond the temporary, refreshing benefit of water, physical water provides a constant reminder of the life that Christ has provided for us.

Science Demonstration

Water possesses many unique and beneficial properties. It is the only chemical that exists at earth temperatures in three different forms: solid ice, liquid, and vapor or humidity. All three forms of water are essential for a healthy earth. Other unusual and important water properties include its dissolving ability, its surface tension, and its expansion.

This particular demonstration shows the large heat capacity of water. Liquid water is able to absorb and give off immense quantities of heat. In this way it moderates the temperature of the entire earth. The moon, with no air or water, has a daytime temperature of 200° F, and drops down to –200° F at night.

Begin this activity by asking the audience what happens when an inflated balloon is placed in a candle flame, and then show

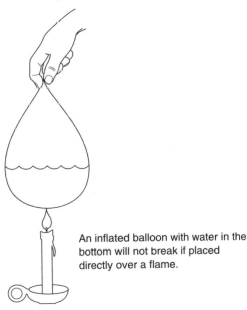

An inflated balloon with water in the bottom will not break if placed directly over a flame.

them: Bang! Next, hold up another balloon that is about one-quarter filled with water and inflated. When it is held in the candle flame, the balloon remains whole. The heat moves into the water so rapidly that the rubber membrane will not burn. Show the group that the balloon has become blackened on the bottom. Make sure that the flame contacts only the water-filled portion of the balloon. This demonstration can actually be continued until the water boils. A water-filled paper cup (not styrofoam) or plastic bag can be substituted for the water-filled balloon.

The demonstration shows how water is designed with unusual heat-holding properties that keep the earth's temperature comfortable. Water is a gift that is valuable in many other ways besides for quenching thirst. Likewise, salvation is a gift that we cannot fully understand but should certainly appreciate and accept.

Science Explanation

This demonstration shows water's unusual ability to store a large amount of heat. Here are some comparative values of heat capacity for various other liquids:

Substance	Heat capacity (cal/gm- °C)
Acetone (C_3H_6O)	.506
Ethyl alcohol (C_2H_5OH)	.54
Liquid mercury (Hg)	.033
Sulfuric acid (H_2SO_4)	.27
Water (H_2O)	1.0

Water, with a value of 1.0, has the largest heat capacity in this list. The physical properties of water are not accidental but designed by the Creator.